Ready for Life

Book One:

How to Be a Good Friend

VICTOR BOOKS

A DIVISION OF SCRIPTURE PRESS PUBLICATIONS INC.
USA CANADA ENGLAND

Ready for Life

Book One:

How to Be a Good Friend

Karen Dockrey

Kevin Johnson

Bob Krafft

Greg Lafferty

Tom Nummela

Mark Oestreicher

Ginny Olson

Dave Veerman, Series Editor

Titles in This Series:
How to Be a Good Friend
How to Get Along with the Opposite Sex
How to Teach Your Parents
How to Win in Life
How to Know What God Wants
How to Explain What You Believe

This book was produced with the assistance of The Livingstone Corporation, David R. Veerman, Daryl J. Lucas, Claudia Gerwin, and Brenda James Todd, project staff.

Structural Editing: David R. Veerman

Copyediting: Daryl J. Lucas, Claudia Gerwin

Cover Design: Joe DeLeon

Typesetting: Brenda James Todd

ISBN: 1-56476-091-X

Contents

READY FOR LIFE

Contributors

Karen Dockrey has served two churches as minister of youth. She currently spends her professional time writing for youth and their leaders. Karen is the author of over fifteen books, including *The Holman Student Bible Dictionary* (Holman) and *The Youth Worker's Guide to Creative Bible Study* (Victor Books). She earned her M.Div. from Southern Baptist Theological Seminary and currently works with youth at Bluegrass Baptist Church in Hendersonville, Tennessee.

Kevin Johnson is the Associate Pastor for Junior High at Elmbrook Church in Waukesha, Wisconsin. He is the author of the junior high devotionals, *Can I Be a Christian Without Being Weird* (Bethany House) and *Why is God Looking for Friends?* (Bethany House). Kevin received his B.A. in English and Print Journalism from University of Wisconsin/River Falls, and his M.Div. from Fuller Theological Seminary.

Bob Krafft is the Campus Life/JV coordinator for Northwest Indiana Youth for Christ in Auburn, Indiana. He has written training and curriculum materials for Youth for Christ/USA and serves as the national Campus Life/JV director for YFC/USA. Bob has his bachelor degrees in Bible and in Business Administration from Fort Wayne Bible College.

Greg Lafferty is pastor to Junior High students at Saddleback Valley Community Church in Mission Viejo, California. He was most recently Pastor to Junior Highers at Wheaton Bible Church in Wheaton, Illinois for several years. Previously, he wrote junior high Sunday School materials for Scripture Press. Greg graduated from Wheaton College in 1984 with a B.A. in Christian Education.

Tom Nummela is editor, writer, and director of Christian Education in the Lutheran Church (Missouri Synod). He has written Sunday School material for junior high-aged young people and preteens, and currently, he is editing high school Bible study materials. Tom earned his B.A. in Arts and Music and his Lutheran Director of Christian Education Certificate from Concordia College (Seward, Nebraska). He also received his Master of Church Music degree from Concordia University (River Forest, Illinois).

Mark Oestreicher is Junior High Pastor at Lake Avenue Congregational Church in Pasadena, California and has been a pastor of young teens for over seven years. He has written or contributed to over 10 books, including *Flex Sessions* (Victor Books). In addition, Mark has published articles in six magazines. Previously, he was a young teen curriculum editor at Scripture Press. Mark earned his B.A. in Christian Education from Wheaton College, Wheaton, Illinois and his M.A. in Educational Ministries from Wheaton Graduate School.

Ginny Olson serves as Assistant Director of Sunlight Express, the Junior High ministry of Willow Creek Community Church in South Barrington, Illinois. She also serves as Editor of *Journey*, a newsletter for women in youth ministry. Ginny received her B.A. in Biblical and Theological Studies from Bethel College, St. Paul, Minnesota, and her M.A. in Educational Ministries from Wheaton Graduate School, Wheaton, Illinois.

Editor

Dave Veerman worked for 26 years for Youth for Christ, and currently is Vice President and Partner in The Livingstone Corporation. For the past several years, he has worked with junior highers at the Naperville Presbyterian Church in Naperville, Illinois and at Hill Middle School through Campus Life/JV. Dave has authored more than 25 books, including *Youth Evangelism* (Victor Books), *Reaching Kids Before High School* (Victor Books), *Small Group Ministry with Youth* (Victor Books), *Video Movies Worth Watching* (Baker Book House), and *How to Apply the Bible* (Tyndale House). He also served as the General Editor for the *Life Application Bible for Students* (Tyndale House). Dave has his B.A. in Bible from Wheaton College and his M.Div. from Trinity Evangelical Divinity School.

WELCOME TO *READY FOR LIFE!*

These meetings are designed to teach junior high students biblically-based life skills. Early adolescents face dramatic changes physically, socially, spiritually, mentally, and emotionally. Life can be confusing as they transform from children into young adults. During this time, they are learning much about themselves and the world. And they are dealing with the strong desire to feel competent—to be good at something. In other words, they want to learn skills, the "how to's." That's why kids this age will sign up for lessons, clinics, camps, and teams for sports, music, and other skills-based activities. At the same time, they are facing the challenges of "growing up." In other words, they now have a whole set of life skills that they need to learn in order to function well in society. These skills range from knowing how to relate to the opposite sex to knowing how to communicate with adults.

With such a strong emphasis on competence, it only makes sense that curriculum and other materials designed for this age group emphasize the teaching of skills. That's why we created *Ready for Life*. Each book in this series contains six meetings focusing on a specific life skill, a skill needed by junior highers as they grow and mature. By definition, a skill is a "how to." So learning a skill means learning "how to" do something. Thus, each of the life skills in *Ready for Life* will begin with those important words . . . how to.

Four basic steps are necessary in teaching *any* skill: explanation (in which the teacher explains the skill), demonstration (in which the teacher demonstrates the skill), supervision (in which students practice the skill under the watchful eye of the teacher), and implementation (in which students practice the skill on their own). In *Ready for Life*, these skill-teaching steps are found in the following sections of each meeting: BIBLE SEARCH (explanation), DEMONSTRATION (demonstration), PRACTICE (supervision), and ASSIGNMENT (implementation).

As we wrote these meetings, we also kept in mind other characteristics of early adolescents, including their short attention span and their tendency to think in concrete terms. Therefore, each meeting is designed to be *fun, creative, fast-moving, concrete,* and *practical.* In addition, these meetings center on the Bible; that is, the life skill being taught flows from a principle of Scripture—these are Christian and biblical life skills.

Another important rule we followed as we designed and wrote is that the meetings had to be volunteer-friendly. All the recommended props and other materials are cheap and easy to find, and no meeting requires expensive or sophisticated equipment. And every page includes plenty of space for you to write your own thoughts, adaptations, and plans. Go ahead—write in the book!

Each meeting is divided into the following parts:

Objective—the desired result of the meeting; the part of the life skill being taught

Materials Needed—the props and other materials that the leader-teacher should gather before the meeting

Opener—an opening game, tied to the theme of the meeting, designed to be fun and to get all the kids involved (about 5 minutes)

Review—an activity or discussion that reviews the content and the assignment from the previous meeting (2-3 minutes)

Starter—a game that introduces the topic of the meeting and gets kids thinking, talking about, and feeling the need for learning the skill (about 5 minutes)

Bible Search—a close look at Scripture—through discussion, small groups, worksheets, or short talks—to discover the life skill (7-10 minutes)

Demonstration—a demonstration by the leader-teacher of how the skill works, using role plays, case studies, and personal stories (7-10 minutes)

Practice—supervised practice by students of the life skill just explained and demonstrated (7-10 minutes)

Assignment—a specific task for students to do on their own during the week to help them implement the life skill (2-3 minutes)

Surprise—an activity, game, or treat to end the meeting with fun and excitement (about 5 minutes)

We have also included **Extras**, other ideas for enhancing the teaching and fun of the meeting. Each meeting takes about 45 minutes, but can be expanded by adding Extras.

I must also add that the creators and writers of *Ready for Life* are highly qualified men and women, from a wide range of church backgrounds, geography, and personal experience. They know kids; they know what they are talking about; and they know youth ministry. Check out their credentials on the previous pages.

Having said that, remember that only *you* know *your* group of students. All the activities in this book should work well with most junior highers, but even the best of them will not necessarily always work with all students. Feel free to adapt this material to suit the unique needs of your group. Again, only you know your kids—trust your judgment.

Well, that's about all I can think to tell you about this series. I pray that God will use these materials to help you reach kids and help you prepare them to be *Ready for Life*.

Dave Veerman, Series Editor

P.S. Check out *Reaching Kids Before High School* (Victor Books). I think you will find it to be a valuable resource.

FRIENDS FOREVER

OBJECTIVE

As a result of this meeting, students will understand the importance of being a good friend.

MATERIALS

- ☐ Bibles
- ☐ Bingo Blast cards (from the "Bingo Blast" worksheet) (OPENER)
- ☐ Pens/pencils (OPENER, PRACTICE)
- ☐ Marker board or chalkboard and markers/chalk (DEMONSTRATION)
- ☐ Index cards (PRACTICE)

For junior highers, friendships are everything

OPENER
Bingo Blast

Pass out pencils and Bingo Blast cards (photocopied from the "Bingo Blast" worksheet) and explain that the students should get the initials of other students who fit each description. A person may initial each Bingo card only once. The goal is to get five boxes initialed in a row up, down, or diagonally. All initialed boxes must be validated by a judge before prizes can be awarded. Collect the cards of the first three students to get Bingo and quickly go through each description to prove that the people fit.

DISCUSSION STARTERS
Works of Art

Explain that everyone will have the opportunity to use his or her artistic talents. You aren't looking for any great works of art, but you do want them to be creative. Tell everyone to flip over their Bingo cards and draw a picture of their good friends in a way that illustrates or symbolizes their good friendship qualities. (The drawings can be of real people or of generic friends.) A drawing, for example, could show a person with big ears for a good listener or a huge heart for someone who cares. Get the group started by doing your own drawing on the board.

After giving the students a few minutes to draw, bring the group back together. Ask for volunteers to show and explain their drawings. As they share, list the qualities on the board. Explain that for the next few weeks you'll be talking about how to be a good friend. If the students haven't come up with the four qualities you'll discuss in these sessions (a good friend *invests time with friends, keeps secrets, listens well,* and *stays loyal*), add them to the list. Circle the four key qualities on the list.

Bingo Blast
5 MINUTES

Works of Art
7 MINUTES

<table>
<tr><td>

Small Groups
7 MINUTES

Important Friends
9 MINUTES

</td><td>

Collect pencils (and papers if they will distract students). Leave the list on the board for use later.

Small Groups

Divide into groups of five (with an adult in each group, if possible.) Starting with the person with the darkest eyes, share answers to the following questions.

Note: Give these questions to the whole group one at a time or hand them to the groups on paper.

- What is your name and one of your favorite animals?

- How important are your friends? Are they more important to you than your family? Than your school? Than God?

- Why are friends so important? What do you get from having friends?

- What makes a friend, a close friend, a really good friend?

- How do you get or make good (close) friends.

Note: Preface each question to help students understand what you're about to ask. For example, before asking the first question above, tell who *your* two close friends are and why; then ask the question.

BIBLE SEARCH
Important Friends

Ask: **What would life be like without friends?** (There would be no one to talk to, no one to do stuff with, no one to help when problems hit, no one to celebrate with when things go well.)

Then say something like: **Without other people, there would be no teams such as football, baseball,**

</td></tr>
</table>

and soccer, and you'd have to hunt your own food and build your own hut! Pretty gross, huh?

We can't survive without other people. But it's not enough just to have people around us. It's possible to be in a crowd and feel lonely or alone. It doesn't feel good to walk into a lunchroom or a class and not see anyone we know. We need friends—people who have the qualities we listed on the board.

Explain that the Bible doesn't use the word "friend" or "friendship" very often, but that it has a lot to say about love. Have one of the students read 1 Corinthians 13:4-7 aloud. Ask them to identify friendship qualities in the passage; write them on the board alongside the list you already made.

Then discuss: **How similar are the lists?** Explain that 1 Corinthians 13 is a good list of what we want in a friend.

To wrap up, say: **You may look at that list and see some of your friends there. Or you may look at it and wish you had a friend like that.**

But think for a moment about how closely it describes *you.* **If someone drew a picture of you, how many of those qualities would you have?**

Here's the key: If you want good friends, you need to *be* **a good friend.**

DEMONSTRATION
My Friend and Me

Talk through the Practice part of the lesson (see below) with reference to your friends so students can see what they need to do. List a couple of your close friends on the board and tell students what friendship qualities those friends have and how you identify them.

Next, write your name on the board and list a cou-

My Friend and Me
5 MINUTES

My Friends and Me
5 MINUTES

What Can I Do?
2 MINUTES

Lose Your Friend
5 MINUTES

ple of the friendship qualities that *you* have and how these are evident in your life. Then pick one or two qualities that you personally need to work on and talk about actions you can take this week to become better in those areas.

PRACTICE
My Friends and Me

Hand out index cards and pencils. Have students list one or two of their good friends. Then ask them to list three qualities (from the lists you made on the board earlier) that those friends have. Finally, have everyone turn over their cards and list the friendship qualities that *they* exhibit.

ASSIGNMENT
What Can I Do?

On the same side of the card (see Practice), have students write one quality that they need to work on more as a friend. Then, thinking of specific friends, have them list at least two actions they can take this week to build those qualities. Encourage them to keep the cards with them and to do what they wrote.

SURPRISE
Lose Your Friend

Have students form a circle with their chairs, everyone sitting down facing in. Stand in the middle and explain that **the object is not to be The Idiot Left In The Middle.** The Idiot points to one person in the circle and asks, "Do you love your friends?" That person can answer yes or no. If they answer yes, everyone must scatter and get another seat in the circle. If the answer is no, the Idiot asks: "What kind of friends do you love?" The person can answer with any descriptive phrase, such as: "Friends with brown eyes" or "Friends with white socks" or something similar. *All*

the people described must get up and find another seat. The "Idiot" then tries to get an open seat from the ones vacated.

Important: You will need to help students keep it moving quickly at first until they remember what to ask:

1. Do you love your friends?

   - If Yes—everyone moves, including the one who asked the question

   - If No—go to **2**

2. What kind of friends do you love?

   - Physical description—those people move.

EXTRAS

Starter: Lonely Circles for cliquey groups

Have students stand in tight circles of 10 to 15 facing each other with arms locked. Pick one person out of the circle and explain that the object of the game is *for that person to get into the middle of the circle.* The students in the circle will almost certainly choose to prevent the person from getting in even though you did *not* tell them to do so. After a couple of rounds, ask what the object of the game was, and just point out how we naturally tend to shut people out of our group or clique of friends. Possibly discuss how it feels to be the one on the outside trying to get in.

Surprise
Continued

BINGO BLAST

Get initials of people who match the description in each square. Try to get five in a row up, down, or diagonally. Each person may initial your card only once.

Someone with same color pants as you	Someone who can recite Romans 3:23	Someone picking his or her nose	Someone who is barefoot	Someone wearing a necklace
Someone who walked to church today	Someone wearing cologne or perfume right now	Someone who is double-jointed	Someone wearing a Christian tee shirt	Someone holding a Bible
Someone with a birthday in the same month as yours	Someone who gives you his or her candy or gum	**FREE FRIEND**	Someone with the same color eyes as you	Someone wearing lipstick
Someone who will sing "Jesus Loves Me"	Someone with a picture of a sibling in his or her wallet	Someone whose hair is shoulder length or longer	Someone who did NOT brush his or her teeth this morning	Someone with a brother or sister in this group
Someone wearing glasses	Someone not wearing deodorant	Someone whose family has cars	Someone who can curl his or her tongue	Someone with a picture of a boyfriend or girlfriend

HOW TO BE A GOOD FRIEND—
MEETING TWO

A GOOD INVESTMENT

OBJECTIVE

As a result of this meeting, students will learn how to invest time in their friends.

MATERIALS

- [ ] Bibles
- [ ] A Newspaper with stock market tables and markers, one each for every three to five students (OPENER)
- [ ] Prizes (OPENER)
- [ ] Marker board or chalk board and markers/chalk (OPENER)
- [ ] Copies of "Investment Report" worksheet (DEMONSTRATION)
- [ ] Pens/pencils (DEMONSTRATION)
- [ ] Copies of "Big Spender" worksheet (PRACTICE)

Friendship

pays

great

dividends

OPENER
Check Your Investment

Divide into groups of three to five and hand out newspapers and markers to each group. Explain that you are going to list different companies on the board, with a number by each one. Their job is to use these company names and numbers to crack a secret code.

Here's how they should do it:

1. Find the company's abbreviation in the newspaper.

2. Note the number that you wrote next to the company name on the board.

3. Count that number of entries down the stock market table.

4. Note the first letter of the company code they land on. This is the first letter in the secret message they're decoding.

5. Repeat with the next company until they've done this with all the company names you listed on the board.

Explain that when the letters are put in the right order, they spell out something.

Important: Prepare this ahead of time by choosing companies and adding numbers that will make up the words "invest time" or "friendship." Make your list using each company's full name and then a number.

Give prizes to the winning group.

REVIEW
S.K.I.L.

Remind students that the topic is friendship. Ask for volunteers to tell how they did at practicing the

What's the Payoff?
5 MINUTES

qualities of being a good friend (the assignment from the last meeting). Last week they agreed that having quality friendships is very important and they began to learn the S.K.I.L. of friendship. (Write S.K.I.L. down the left side of the board.) Explain that each letter stands for a skill in building good friendships, and that today they are going to learn the "I" in S.K.I.L., which stands for Investing time. (You won't be studying these skills in order.)

DISCUSSION STARTER
What's the Payoff?

Ask: **What does it mean to invest?** Allow for individual answers. Explain that to have good friends we need to learn to *invest* time in them rather than just *spend* time with them. Just as we can invest money, spend money, and sometimes waste money, the same is true with friendship. We can invest time that builds friendship; and we can spend or waste time that contributes nothing or even damages friendship.

Have students name activities they do with friends (such as play sports, go to church, hang out, stay all night, talk, etc.). List these activities down one side of the board. Then go through the list and write the payoff for each activity. Answers could include:

Activity	Payoff
Play basketball	Become physically fit
Go to church	Gain strength through fellowship; grow spiritually
Watch TV	Spend time; be entertained
Talk about things	Deepen friendship
Share hurts	Gain emotional help
Study together	Develop mental sharpness; improve grades
Play video games	Spend time; be entertained

Look through the list and ask which activities have the best payoff and which ones bring them closer to their friends.

BIBLE SEARCH
Put Your Spurs On

Have a student read Hebrews 10:23-25 aloud. Ask how Christians can "spur one another on toward love and good deeds" (verse 24). If students struggle to answer, explain that they can do those activities that have good payoffs. Helping each other physically, spiritually, mentally, and emotionally is far better than just spending time.

Read verse 25 again and ask why friends might quit meeting together. After a few answers, explain that friendships that involve merely having fun together now and then don't build close relationships. But the people with whom we do the harder things (such as sharing who we really are, talking about problems, or even working on a project) become investments.

Those friendships really last and become a source of encouragement.

DEMONSTRATION
Limited Time

Explain that each person has 168 hours in a week. Only some of that time can be spent with friends.

Everyone in the group will now get to analyze how they spend time with friends—in the same way that an investor looks at his or her investments—to see whether they're getting a good return on their investments.

Hand out pencils and copies of the Investment Report worksheet. Have everyone fill out one copy.

Put Your Spurs On
7 MINUTES

Limited Time
10 MINUTES

After five minutes, discuss the worksheet. Ask volunteers to show their totals for each kind of time. Talk about what kinds of time are good investments in friends.

PRACTICE
Big Spender

Introduce this activity by explaining that though it takes time and effort to invest in friends, the payoff makes it worth the trouble. Then have the group break into pairs. Each student should be with someone he or she doesn't know very well so that they can meaningfully answer the questions on the Big Spender worksheet. (Add other questions you want your students to discuss.) Have each pair answer $10 worth of questions.

After a few minutes, pull everyone back together and discuss:

- **What questions were the most difficult to answer? Why?**

- **Which ones are the most important to answer? Why?**

ASSIGNMENT
Invest in Them!

On the bottom of their Big Spender worksheets, have students each write the name of one friend they want to invest in. They should write down two things they plan to do this week to invest in them.

SURPRISE
Check Them Out!

This activity requires that you or another adult

Big Spender
8 MINUTES

Invest in Them!
2 MINUTES

Check Them Out!
5 MINUTES

leader watch during the meeting for kids investing in their friends—encouraging others, working hard at the discussion questions, being kind, etc.

At this point in the meeting, thank everyone for working hard on such a tough subject and tell them you want to reward a few students whom you noticed making friendship investments during the meeting. Give a candy bar as a way of recognizing each investor. Explain to the group what each person did (or whisper to the prize winners what you noticed).

EXTRA
Shoe Exchange

For the active group. Explain that you have been talking about the stock exchange, and now you're going to do something a little different—the shoe exchange. Divide into teams and line up the teams at one end of the room. Take one person from each team and send him or her to the other end of the room. This is the Waiting Person. The first person in line in each team should run to the other end of the room, switch one shoe with the person waiting, and stay there to become the new Waiting Person. Then, the person who *used* to be the Waiting Person should run back and tag the next person in line. That person, then, should run down and switch one shoe with the Waiting Person, and so on, until all have run through the relay. When the last person has switched shoes, both should run back to the rest of the team. Then they *all* must get their own shoes back and put them on. The first team to finish, wins.

Surprise
Continued

INVESTMENT REPORT

Three steps:

1. What do you do in a week with friends? Fill in STUFF YOU DO.

2. How much time do you spend at each? Guesstimate how much TIME YOU SPEND for each activity.

3. What kind of time is each activity? (KIND OF TIME— active time, class time, goof-off time, media time, help time, talk time, spiritual growth time).

STUFF YOU DO:

TIME YOU SPEND:

KIND OF TIME:

To think about: Do you spend a lot of time in one area and not much in another? (Are you too serious? Are you too goofy?)

BIG SPENDER

$1 questions:

- How many people are in your family? Who are they?

- What pets do you have?

- What is your favorite sport?

$2 questions:

- What do you like to do in your free time?

- Why do you attend church?

- What's your favorite class at school?

- What do you want to do when you grow up?

$3 questions:

- What are you afraid of?

- If you could change one thing in your family, what would you change?

- How did you become a Christian?

SHHH! IT'S A SECRET

OBJECTIVE

As a result of this meeting, students will see the importance of keeping secrets that their friends entrust to them.

The secret to great friendships

MATERIALS

- ☐ Bibles
- ☐ $1 bill (OPENER)
- ☐ Marker board or chalkboard and markers/chalk (REVIEW)
- ☐ Secrets (DISCUSSION STARTER)
- ☐ Questions for small group practice (PRACTICE)
- ☐ Prizes (SURPRISE)
- ☐ Paper (EXTRAS)
- ☐ Pens/pencils (EXTRAS)

OPENER
Bill

Before the meeting, secretly give a dollar bill to a student and tell him or her to put it in his or her pocket and not tell anyone about it.

Open the meeting by informing the group that you have given somebody a dollar. The person who discovers whom you gave it to gets to keep it.

After a few minutes (or after the dollar is found), discuss what happened. How did the person keep or lose the dollar? Did he or she lie to cover up that he or she had it? Did the person say anything misleading? If the dollar was found, what gave the person away? Explain to the group that the topic of this meeting is *keeping secrets*.

REVIEW
S.K.I.L.

Write "S.K.I.L." down the left side of the board. Ask students to explain what S.K.I.L. refers to and the letter you talked about last week. (It refers to the fact that friendship is a *skill* that we can learn; the I stands for *investing* time and energy in friends.) Remind students that friendship just doesn't happen—it takes *work* and *skill,* such as investing time with friends, and doing activities that aren't just fun but that also last and build friendship.

Then ask volunteers to share what they did this past week to invest in their friendships.

DISCUSSION STARTER
I've Got a Secret

Before you begin the meeting, tell a fake secret to

Bill
5 MINUTES

S.K.I.L.
3 MINUTES

I've Got a Secret
5 MINUTES

one of the first students to arrive—not the same person who received the dollar, and someone who is a good sport. Explain clearly that you *don't* want the student to share the secret, but make your secret juicy enough to make it hard to keep. Here are some possible secrets:

- From a paid youth worker: "The church is out of money and my position is being cut."
- From a volunteer: "I was promoted at work, so I won't be able to work with the group anymore."
- An activity has been canceled
- "I got a speeding ticket on my way here."
- Somebody's birthday is today
- A leader is engaged to be married
- Two of the leaders had a big fight

After the review, explain to the students that you have an announcement to make about _______ (the secret). Ask how many of the students have heard it. If no one has, explain what you did and congratulate the person who kept the secret. If any students raise their hands, just explain that it wasn't true. Your point isn't to make the student who spread the secret feel bad, but to see how well the group keeps a secret and to demonstrate to them how quickly a secret can spread. Explain that you set someone up and that it's difficult for you to keep secrets too.

Write "Keep secrets" after **K** in S.K.I.L. and explain that keeping secrets is an important part of being a good friend.

BIBLE SEARCH
Gossip

Discuss:

- **How do you feel when someone betrays a secret of yours? (Probably angry, hurt.)**

- **What causes *you* to share secrets that someone has entrusted to you? See what students say. If they're like most people, they probably felt it was justified.**

Discuss each question briefly. Then say something like: **Sometimes we tell secrets from genuine concern, but most of the time it's to put someone down or to gain popularity. Sometimes we pretend as though we're sharing prayer requests . . . and then never pray. That's gossip.**

It's obvious that we won't have good friendships if we can't keep secrets. Let's look at a short verse on keeping secrets.

Have a student read Proverbs 11:13 aloud: "A gossip betrays a confidence, but a trustworthy man keeps a secret" (NIV). Then ask the following questions and discuss each one briefly:

- **What is a gossip?** (A person who spreads personal or sensational facts for self-serving reasons)

- **What does "confidence" mean as it's used in Proverbs 11:13?** (A trust)

- **What does it mean to be trustworthy?** (People can count on you)

Then continue: **When people tell their secrets, they tell us "in confidence"—with confidence that the information won't go any farther. If we gossip and don't keep secrets, we betray people (that's like Judas betraying Jesus—nasty stuff). The opposite**

Gossip
10 MINUTES

happens when we keep a secret—we build trust between each other. Then we can share deeper concerns—our hurts, our hopes, difficult circumstances at home—and get the support we need from friends.

Important: Telling the students to keep secrets needs qualification. Ask the students when they *shouldn't* keep secrets. There are times when people should tell secrets that have been entrusted to them, even if they promised not to tell. The most obvious example is whenever someone will be hurt, such as whenever a person:

- hints at or threatens suicide

- is going to commit a severe crime

- is involved in sexual or physical abuse as a victim or perpetrator

If you haven't talked about these topics with your group, suggest whom they should tell—police, counselors, pastors, parents, a mental health crisis line, or whoever else is most appropriate.

DEMONSTRATION
Keeping Secrets

Tell the group that you want to talk about keeping secrets in everyday life. On the board list the group's responses (and/or the suggested responses) to the following questions:

- **What could the person with the dollar (earlier in the meeting) have done if people had tried to corner him (or her) into telling?** After a brief discussion, give these possible responses: Lying isn't OK, so you might say "It isn't any of your business," "I wouldn't tell you," "I can't say," "I'm not sure," or "Go ask them." Explain that saying, "I know but I can't tell" is just inviting pressure to tell the secret.

Keeping Secrets
7 MINUTES

- **What can you do when you know something juicy, like the person who knew the fake secret?** After a brief discussion, give these possible responses: Don't listen in the first place; ask yourself if you would want the secret spread if the secret were about you; do something productive—ask if you can help, pray, or tell a parent, counselor, teacher, or pastor if they need to know.

PRACTICE

Groups

Break into small groups of ten or less, each with an adult leader. Have the groups answer the following questions (give these questions to your group leaders). Remind the groups that they can look at your list on the board for ideas.

- Someone asks you if it's true that a friend isn't a virgin. She is. What do you do?

- You're the only person at school who knows that a girl you can't stand just broke up with the most popular boy at school. What do you do?

- At a meeting someone plugged the toilet and flooded the bathroom. You know who did it. What do you do?

- Your older sister sneaks out in the middle of the night to meet an older guy. What do you do?

- A friend tells you that life is really depressing and sometimes he wishes he were dead. What do you do?

Groups
8 MINUTES

<table>
<tr><td>

Blabber Mouth
2 MINUTES

Pump It Out
5 MINUTES

</td><td>

ASSIGNMENT
Blabber Mouth

Give each student the name of a different animal. Be sure to write down who has what animal. Explain that they must keep their animals a total secret until next week—*no telling anybody!* (At next week's meeting, you'll see who knows whose animals.)

SURPRISE
Pump It Out

Before the meeting, hide a few treats, prizes, or refreshments somewhere in the room. Explain that the students have a chance to see how well *you* can keep a secret. They can ask questions about the location of the treats, etc., but that you will answer only yes or no. See how many questions it takes them to find each surprise.

EXTRAS
Hide-N-Seek

This activity can be done in a large or small group. Either way, give some of the students a secret, written down on slips of paper or whispered to them. The other students should then ask questions of the students who have the secret. The students with the secret must answer all questions without lying. See how long they can keep the secret. Take turns with who knows the secret and who asks the questions until your time for this part of the meeting is up.

Secrets could include:

- Announcements of upcoming events or trips

- Someone's birthday

- A little-known fact about a staff member

</td></tr>
</table>

- A funny story or tongue twister

Hot-n-Cold

Play the old child's game called "Hot and Cold." This is the game in which one person thinks of something in the room that the others must try to find. The only clues they have are the words "Cold," "Warm," and "Hot." The searchers move around the room, and the person who knows what the object is reports on whether they're cold, warm, or hot, depending on how close they are to it. (Jokesters like to add a couple more categories, "Very Hot," "Red Hot," "White Hot," "Ultra-Mega Hot," and "Cosmically Hot." Add categories as you like, but cut it off at "Ultra-Mega Hot" for safety purposes.)

When students think they know what the object is, give them one guess as a group. If they are right, they get a point. If they are wrong, *you* get a point. Play until your time is up or until a predetermined score is reached.

Extras
Continued

HOW TO BE A GOOD FRIEND—
MEETING FOUR

LEND ME YOUR EARS

OBJECTIVE

As a result of this meeting, students will be good listeners to their friends.

MATERIALS

- [ ] Bibles
- [ ] Chalkboard or marker board and markers/chalk (REVIEW, BIBLE SEARCH)
- [ ] Prizes (EXTRAS)

The importance of listening

OPENER
Lend Me Your Ear

Have students sit in lines of ten to fifteen students each (form at least two teams, even if each has only a few students). Whisper a story, Bible verse, or saying to the first person in each line. Tell that person, in turn, to whisper what he or she heard to the next person in his or her line, so on down to the last person. The last person in each line should share aloud what he or she heard. The funnier the story or the more difficult the saying, the crazier the final result will be. Stories or sayings could include:

- The ants in France fall mainly in your pants.

- The big black bug bit the big brown bear and the big brown bear bled blue blood.

- Seven Sicilian sailors sailed the seven seas on sausages and salami.

- "He who answers before listening—that is his folly and his shame" (Proverbs 18:13, NIV).

- "He who listens to you listens to me; he who rejects you rejects me; but he who rejects me rejects Him who sent me" (Luke 10:16, NIV).

REVIEW
Secret Animal Review

Ask who learned others' secret animals from last week. If very few did, congratulate everyone for doing a good job of keeping their secrets. If students learned a lot of the animals, encourage everyone to work harder on keeping secrets.

Next, write S.K.I.L. on the board and review the letters you've discussed so far: **I** = *Invest Time in Friendships,* and **K** = *Keep Secrets.* Have students explain each

---

Lend Me Your Ear
5 MINUTES

Secret Animal Review
3 MINUTES

"I Have . . ."
5 MINUTES

point. Then see if they can guess, from the opening game, the topic of *this* meeting (listening). When they guess, write "Listen" on the board next to the L in S.K.I.L.

DISCUSSION STARTER
"I Have . . ."

Explain that you're going to test everyone's listening skills. Seat students in a circle facing each other. Have the person whose birthday is closest to today start by saying "I have . . ." and then put in a noun or short phrase that is true about him or her. It could be an animal, food, object, sickness, condition, etc. Going clockwise, the next person in the circle should repeat what the last person said and add something new. Each person in turn should repeat what was said last and add something else. Keep going until someone makes a mistake. Then start over with that person.

Some possible things to add:

- bad breath
- a cat
- a watermelon
- a mother
- a fudge bar
- a contact lens in my eye
- a toothbrush
- a ball
- a toothache
- a Bible verse memorized
- a zit on my nose
- to go to the bathroom
- a new Bible

Note: You may need to give some suggestions to get the students going, but be sure that they don't just go down your list.

Throughout the game, compliment students on being good listeners.

BIBLE SEARCH
Are You Listening?

After a few minutes, stop the game and compliment everyone on how well they did. Then say something like: **It isn't always important to listen to tongue twisters or weird lists. But it's *very* important to listen well to each other. After all, we don't like it when people don't listen to us.**

How do you know someone isn't listening to you? List answers on the board as students give their ideas. Also ask:

- What body language shows that a person isn't listening?

- What words show that a person isn't listening?

- What actions show that a person isn't listening?

Then say something like: **It really hurts when people don't listen to us. It's as though we don't exist.**

It isn't hard to learn to be a good listener. And if you have a head it's easy to remember three things you need to do to be a good listener.

Have a student read James 1:19 aloud. Ask: **What does James say we should do to be good listeners?** (Be quick to listen and slow to speak.)

Draw a head on the board with big ears and a closed, little mouth. Explain that being good listeners means *keeping our mouths shut.* You may want to address specific habits you see among your students— talking when someone up front is talking,

Are You Listening?
7 MINUTES

interrupting, nonstop chattering, etc.—and point out that these actions get in the way of listening to people.

Explain that listening also includes *opening our ears*. It doesn't do much good to keep our mouths shut if we don't really concentrate on what someone is saying. At school it's easy for the mind to wander. But if we do that in a conversation, we aren't really listening.

Explain that one more thing should be added to the drawing. Draw big eyes on the face on the board, and say: **We need to *look people in the eye* when we listen. Why do we need to do that? It's hard to look people in the eye (whether they're teachers, parents, or friends) because it can feel uncomfortable. But looking at a person makes him or her feel listened to, and that's what we want to do for our friends.**

To wrap up, ask everyone to tell you what three things make a good listener. Then explain that next there will be a demonstration of listening skills.

DEMONSTRATION
The Bad and the Good

Before your meeting, arrange for two people (adults or students) to role-play a conversation in front of the group. The first person, the Talker, should try to share something significant—how he or she became a Christian, a problem at school or work or at home, or trouble with a friend. The second person, the Listener, should display bad listening skills, such as:

- Problem solving—"Have you thought about trying. . . ."

- "I was in that situation once and this is what happened. . . ."

- Changes the subject—"Oh really? By the way, have you heard about . . . ?"

The Bad and the Good
10 MINUTES

- Doesn't pay attention—"Huh? What did you say?"

- Doesn't look at speaker—looks at watch, looks behind the person speaking, picks lint off speaker's shirt, bends down and ties own shoe, bends down and ties speaker's shoe, etc.

The speaker can show frustration *but should keep talking*. Then the Listener should walk away while the speaker is still talking. Once the conversation is finished, ask students to point out what the Listener did wrong. Be sure to highlight the three listening skills—(1) keep your mouth shut, (2) look the person in the eye, (3) keep eyes open (be attentive).

Bring both people back to the front and have them discuss the same topic again. This time, however, the Listener should display good listening skills.

PRACTICE
Who's That?

Get everyone into circles of ten. Have students pair off with one person they don't know well and designate the older person as the listener. The other half of each pair should tell about him- or herself: full name, pets, family members, hobbies, where born, favorite food, favorite color, etc. Remind the listeners to use the skills they've learned: (1) keep your mouth shut, (2) look the person in the eye, (3) be attentive.

After a minute or two, have each listener introduce his or her partner to the rest of his or her group of ten, telling everything he or she can remember about the partner. Have the students being introduced tell what was missed. If you have time, switch roles and repeat the exercise.

Who's That?
8 MINUTES

<table>
<tr><td valign="top" width="38%">

Keeping Track
2 MINUTES

Finish Me Off
5 MINUTES

</td><td valign="top">

ASSIGNMENT
Keeping Track

Tell students to keep track of five conversations they have this week. For each, they should write down how well they followed the three guidelines for listening:

1. Did you keep your mouth shut?

2. Did you keep your ears open?

3. Did you look the person in the eyes?

SURPRISE
Finish Me Off

Have a competition between two teams—guys versus girls, tall versus short, or whatever. Have the teams form two lines facing the front. The first person in each line competes first. No one else on the team is allowed to talk. Tell the students they'll need to listen carefully as you say part of a well-known saying. The first person at the head of each line to give the rest of the sentence wins. Then those two should go to the back of their lines and let the next two compete. Keep score, awarding 100 points for each correct answer. Give the winning team a treat or let them get refreshments first.

Sayings could include:

- He who hesitates (is lost)
- All that glitters (is not gold)
- All's well that (ends well)
- Curiosity (killed the cat)
- The proof of the pudding (is in the eating)
- Don't burn your bridges (behind you)
- Don't count your chickens (before they hatch)
- Where there's a will (there's a way)

</td></tr>
</table>

- Waste not, (want not)
- Haste makes (waste)
- A word to the wise (is sufficient)
- Every cloud has (a silver lining)
- A fool and his money (are soon parted)
- You can't have your cake (and eat it too)
- Too many cooks (spoil the broth)
- Strike while (the iron is hot)
- A watched pot (never boils)
- Birds of a feather (flock together)

EXTRAS
Directions

When you give the group these directions, don't repeat any of them. Say: **Listen carefully and do everything I say.** Then give the following instructions, pausing where indicated:

- **Stand up and face the front.** (pause)
- **Turn around and face the back of the room.** (pause)
- **Take one-half step backwards.** (pause)
- **Touch all four walls with your forehead and then sit facing east.** (pause)
- **Turn to the north and walk to the nearest opening in the wall.** (pause)
- **Ask someone for directions to the closest Pizza Hut and walk five steps in that direction.**

After they have executed the instructions, have everyone sit down right where they are and give a prize to each person who followed the instructions most accurately.

Surprise
Continued

HOW TO BE A GOOD FRIEND—
MEETING FIVE

STAYING CLOSE

OBJECTIVE

As a result of this meeting, students will learn how to stay loyal to their friends.

MATERIALS

- ☐ Bibles
- ☐ Marker board or chalkboard and markers/chalk (REVIEW)
- ☐ Candy (DISCUSSION STARTER)
- ☐ Role-plays (PRACTICE)
- ☐ Index cards (ASSIGNMENT)
- ☐ Pens/pencils (ASSIGNMENT)
- ☐ Grocery bags labeled "Truth" and "Or Else" (SURPRISE)
- ☐ Written questions and gross food items (SURPRISE)
- ☐ Pictures of loyalty (EXTRA)

OPENER
Roll Over, Rover

Have the students get into pairs. Explain that you want to see how loyal they are. Instruct one student in each pair to stand and the other to get down on his or her hands and knees like a dog. Tell the "Dogs" that they have to be loyal and obey their "Masters." Then have the Masters spend a couple of minutes demonstrating pet tricks with their dogs; they can tell them to sit up, roll over, heel, shake hands, beg, etc. If you have time, switch roles. Then restore everyone's dignity and explain that you'll be talking about loyalty during this meeting.

REVIEW
Spell It Out

Review the acrostic your students are using to help them learn the skill of friendship by having four students come up front (S.K.I.L.). Have each student write one of the letters on the board. After each letter, have the person say the word that goes with that letter and explain it. The person who writes the S won't know the answer, but let the group guess a few times. Then introduce the last skill of friendship: *Stay Loyal.*

Ask for volunteers to share what they did to carry out the assignment from last week (to keep track of five conversations they had, noting how well they followed the three guidelines for listening).

DISCUSSION STARTER
Candy Giveaway

Pick a few students and call them up to the front of

Roll Over, Rover
5 MINUTES

Spell It Out
3 MINUTES

Candy Giveaway
5 MINUTES

the room. Give each a candy bar, but explain that they must give the candy away—they cannot eat it. Then, one by one, have them give away their candy bars.

After all the candy is given away, discuss the experience. Ask: **How did you decide who to give your candy bar to?** (Gave it to my best friend; gave it to the loudest person; gave it to the closest person; couldn't decide, so split it between several people; etc.) Point out that sometimes it's hard to know whom to be loyal to.

BIBLE SEARCH
Loyalty

Ask the students if loyalty is like being a dog and doing whatever your master says. Why or why not?

Explain that acting like a dog isn't the only thing we might mistake for loyalty. Ask whether any of the following are real loyalty:

- promising to be best friends forever

- doing dares to join a group

- lying to protect a friend

- pricking fingers, etc. to become "blood brothers"

Explain that we all want friends who will be loyal, who will stick with us and stick up for us. In fact, 1 Corinthians 13:7 says: "If you love someone, you will be loyal to him no matter what the cost" (TLB).

Have someone read Proverbs 18:24 aloud. Then explain that true friends stick "closer than a brother"—they're loyal!

Explain that Christ is our example of real loyalty. Have three students each read a verse of 1 John 3:16-18. Ask: **What does this passage say real loyalty is?** After a few answers, explain that real loyalty shows *un-*

Loyalty
10 MINUTES

selfishness, just as Jesus laid down his life for us. Loyalty, in other words, is much like heroism (like pushing someone out of the way of a bus or a speeding train).

Ask: **What else does 1 John 3:16-18 say about loyalty?** After a few answers, explain that real loyalty is love in action, not just words or dramatic heroism. Loyalty is everyday stuff, such as providing food for someone who is hungry. Loyalty means sticking up for someone and sticking by him or her.

Say: **First John 3:17 points out that loyalty comes from the love of God inside of us. That means that God defines what love and loyalty and what right and wrong are. God wants us to be loyal to friends. We need to remember, though, that our ultimate loyalty belongs to God. It says in Matthew 22:34-40 that we should love God with all our heart, soul, and mind, and our neighbor as ourselves.**

That means that loyalty to friends and loyalty to God sometimes will conflict, such as when a friend wants you to do something wrong.

DEMONSTRATION

Examples

Give the following case studies as examples of students who knew how to stay loyal.

Miguel and Trace

Miguel and Trace are good friends. Recently, Trace has been having trouble in math, Miguel's best subject. Trace has an important test coming up, so he asks Miguel to help him study for it. Miguel would rather watch his favorite TV show, but because of their friendship, he helps Trace study instead. That's loyalty.

**Examples
5 MINUTES**

Gretchen and Cindi

Gretchen and Cindi have been friends since third grade. Cindi is a cheerleader at school and is very popular. Yesterday, one of Cindi's cheer leading friends made fun of Gretchen's outfit behind her back. Instead of going along or being quiet, Cindi said, "Gretchen is a good friend of mine. Please don't put her down." That's loyalty.

Frank and Tony

Because their last names begin with the same letter, Frank and Tony sit near each other in most of their classes. Over the year, they have become pretty good friends. Last week the teacher blamed Tony for something he didn't do. Frank spoke up in Tony's defense, explaining to the teacher that Tony was innocent. That's loyalty.

Repeat the point that loyalty means standing by, sticking with, and standing up for a friend.

PRACTICE
Play It Out

Play It Out
10 MINUTES

Choose six students who are willing to participate in some role-plays. Have them pair up and give each pair a written situation to act out (some possibilities follow—choose ones that fit your group). Allow about two minutes for them to prepare.

While your six actors are preparing, explain to the rest of the group that the biggest problem in being loyal to friends is dealing with conflicting loyalties. Our loyalty to God, our parents, ourselves, and our friends sometimes conflict directly with each other, and we have to choose which gets our greatest loyalty.

When your actors are ready, introduce them. You'll need to do this for each role-play.

Possible role-plays (choose ones that fit your group):

- You have a good friend whom you've known for years. You're just starting to make friends with some very popular students at school. You are standing at lunch with one of these new friends when your old friend walks by. The new, popular friend starts to make fun of your old friend as he or she walks by.

- You are planning to stay overnight at your best friend's house this Friday. You've made plans, and both of you have been looking forward to it for a few weeks. On Thursday you get invited to *the* most popular party in school by some other friends. They won't allow you to bring anyone else, and you really want to go. You are talking to your best friend about it on the phone Thursday night.

- Your parents have grounded you for something you did. It's Friday night and they went out until 11:00 P.M. Your friend comes over and asks you to go with him to the mall until 10:30 P.M.

- You get permission to go to a friend's home overnight. Your parents won't let you go to the big dance at school. Your friend suggests that you come over and then go to the dance anyway and just say you were at his house all night.

- Your *best* friend is asking you to go with him and some others after school to (smoke, steal, or drink, depending on your group). You believe it's wrong, but you don't want to be left out of the group.

- Your *best* friend doesn't really care much about church or Christ. His parents make him go to church, and he despises it. You're a Christian and really want to live for Jesus. Your friend is trying to get you to cut out of church and go play video games.

Practice
Continued

Bring It Back
2 MINUTES

Tell the Truth or Else!
5 MINUTES

Be sure to applaud each group for their efforts and explain that sometimes loyalty requires *tough* choices. Are we going to be loyal to God, ourselves, family, or friends?

ASSIGNMENT
Bring It Back

Hand out index cards and pencils. Have students choose one person they feel they are loyal to and write that person's name on the card. Tell them to use the card to keep track of the ways they were loyal or disloyal to that person this week. Have them bring their cards back next week for a small treat if they have written answers on their cards.

SURPRISE
Tell the Truth or Else!

Have two grocery bags labeled "Truth" and "Or Else." In the Truth bag place slips of paper with questions on them that the students must answer (see list of Truths below, which you may photocopy if you wish). In the Or Else bag, place gross food items they must take out and eat (see list below). Get the students in a circle and place the bags in the center. Have them pass a ball, shoe, or other object around the circle while you play music. When the music stops, the person left holding the object must pick a Truth or Or Else from the bags in the middle of the circle.

Truth

- You find a $5 bill under the pew at church. No one sees it and you have no idea who it belongs to. What would you do?

- You see a friend steal some gum at the grocery store. He hasn't left yet. What do you do?

- You hear two small children using very bad language in the playground. What do you do?

- Your friend asks for the answers on a test at school. What do you do?

- You get an "A" on a big test at school, but when you look at it you see the teacher made a mistake and it should have been a "C." What do you do?

- You buy something and the clerk gives you a $10 bill and two ones instead of the three ones you had coming to you. What do you do?

- You break an expensive decoration at church but no one sees you. What do you do?

- Your friend (that your parents don't really like) stains your mom's new carpet. He or she wants you to take the blame. What do you do?

- You're on the school bus and someone drops a Gameboy under the seat. You find it after the person leaves and no one knows. You've always wanted one. What do you do?

- Your teacher, using the "honor system," asks how many have done their reading for today. She's giving points for those who raise their hands. You usually do your homework but you forgot this time. What do you do?

Or Else!

- small onion (or a large one, and everyone takes a bite)

- baby food

- black olives

- anchovies

- jalapeño pepper

- carrot or tomato juice

- small green tomato

Surprise
Continued

<table>
<tr><td valign="top" style="border:1px solid black; padding:1em; width:30%;">

Surprise
Continued

</td><td valign="top">

- a *very* brown banana

- raw green beans

- cold mashed potatoes

- sardines

EXTRA
Pictures

Beforehand, cut the following pictures of loyalty out of magazines and newspapers: person and dog; husband and wife; parent and child; co-workers; person and country; teammates; friends; soldiers; pastor and church member; etc. Hold the pictures up one at a time and ask: **Why is this a picture of loyalty? How does each person (animal) show his or her loyalty? Where might the loyalty be tested?**

</td></tr>
</table>

STEER RIGHT

OBJECTIVE

As a result of this meeting, students will know that
the most important thing they can do for their friends
is to steer them the right way.

MATERIALS

- [ ] Bibles
- [ ] Marker board or chalkboard and markers/chalk (REVIEW)
- [ ] Treats (REVIEW)
- [ ] Paper (BIBLE SEARCH)
- [ ] Pens/pencils (BIBLE SEARCH)
- [ ] Blindfolds (one for DISCUSSION STARTER; enough for half the group for EXTRA)
- [ ] Picnic goodies and supplies (SURPRISE):
  - bread
  - peanut butter
  - jelly
  - cookies
  - utensils
  - cups
  - drinks

Don't give friends a bum steer

OPENER
Leader Lines

Organize students into lines of five to ten facing the front. Choose your most outgoing students to be the leaders of each group. Explain that this is similar to "Follow the Leader." The groups must stay where they are as the leaders do different movements that everyone down their line must copy. Give examples of what the leaders can do: flapping arms, patting heads, jumping on one leg, putting a finger in an ear, doing the hula, etc. Then tell the leaders to begin. After a couple of minutes, congratulate everyone on the excellent way that they followed their leaders. Then get everyone quiet, seated, and facing the front.

REVIEW
S.K.I.L.

Write "S.K.I.L." vertically on the board and ask who can remember what each letter represents. As students fill in the acrostic, ask how they have put each skill into practice. Focus especially on last meeting's assignment (to use an index card to keep track of the ways they were loyal or disloyal to a specific person). Give treats (as promised) to those who brought their cards, with answers, to the meeting.

DISCUSSION STARTER
Blind Obstacle Course

Pick three students who can take a joke well. Have someone take them to another room. While they're out, explain to the rest of the group that they should play along with you and not let the others know what's happening. Then clear an aisle through the room and place obstacles such as pillows, books, chairs, small tables, etc. in the way.

Leader Lines
5 MINUTES

S.K.I.L.
3 MINUTES

Blind Obstacle Course
5 MINUTES

Bring the students back in the room one at a time and explain that all they need to do is complete the obstacle course blindfolded by following the lead of another student. Put the blindfold on the first victim and choose a leader from the audience. The leader can give only verbal commands such as "right," "left," "lift your leg up," "jump," "step over," etc. The trick is that after the person has been blindfolded, you should quietly remove all the obstacles and make him or her jump, step, and move over nothing.

After each person has finished the course, remove the blindfold and reveal the obstacle-free course. Then congratulate the person on doing such a good job and on being a good sport.

BIBLE SEARCH
Sharpen Up

Read Proverbs 27:17 aloud—"As iron sharpens iron, so one man sharpens another" (NIV). Ask how iron sharpens iron and how that relates to friendship. Explain by saying something like: **Think about two large knives as they rub together sharpening one another. The abrasion and friction cause the edges to become sharp. The same is true with friendship. The rough times often cause friendship to grow the most. Challenging a friend to do the right thing can be scary, but it usually pays off.**

It goes both ways too. Sometimes you need to be willing to be sharpened or challenged by your friends. One knife doesn't do all the sharpening. Both knives sharpen each other.

Answer this question to yourself: *Am I helping others along or holding them back?* **As a friend, you can help others get closer to God, get closer to family, do better in school, and look good. Or, you can hold them back by your lack of concern or lack of exam-**

Sharpen Up
10 MINUTES

ple. **If you have a strong walk with Christ, your life will influence your friends in their daily lives, helping them in their relationship with Jesus. In the same way, if you make certain to hang with at least some people who have a good walk with the Lord, they will help sharpen your life.**

After discussing Proverbs 27:17, break into small groups of eight to ten students, each with an adult leader. Give each group a sheet of paper and a pen/pencil to record their answers. Have a student read 2 Timothy 2:22 aloud to the group. Explain that this verse lists four areas where we can steer our friends the right way—righteousness, faith, love, and peace (NIV).

Explain: **As a small group, brainstorm ways you can pursue God's best in righteousness, faith, love, and peace. In other words, how can you and your friends pursue those things?** Someone from each group should record the group's answers. You'll discuss them in the Demonstration exercise that follows.

DEMONSTRATION

Answers

Have the groups report what they decided in each of the four areas. Following are some possible answers; supplement their answers with any ideas you think might help.

- **How can you and friends pursue *righteousness?*** (Help friends decide and choose to do what's right; warn each other when we're about to blow it; keep language and behavior clean.)

- **How can you and friends pursue *faith?*** (Make sure you all get to church; don't be afraid to let people know you're Christians; make Christian friends a priority.)

Answers
5 MINUTES

- **How can you and friends pursue *love?*** (Help each other with chores and homework; be servants to each other.)

- **How can you and friends pursue *peace?*** (Don't gossip, don't cause fights between friends.)

Note: You may need to define each word before you discuss its application.

PRACTICE
Fold It and Pass It

Have everyone get back into their small groups. Form the groups in circles and pass out a sheet of paper and a pen or pencil to each person. Have each person write his or her name at the *bottom* of the paper. Explain that everyone should pass his or her paper to the person on the right, who should write a short statement of encouragement at the very top. When everyone has finished writing, they should fold the top down over what they have written and pass the paper on to their right. Each person in the circle should write on everyone else's paper until the papers all come back to their owners. When this happens, give students time to read through their papers.

Then comment on how good it feels to have friends who encourage you. Challenge students to show the same concern and encouragement throughout the week with their friends.

ASSIGNMENT
Encourage One Another

Thank the students for encouraging each other and for helping build stronger friendships over the past few weeks. Their assignment during this next week is

Fold It and Pass It
10 MINUTES

Encourage One Another
2 MINUTES

to encourage two other people, just as they did in the encouragement sheets (during Practice). They can write notes or just say something encouraging.

SURPRISE
Silent Picnic

Explain that refreshments will be served, but that everyone will have to work together to get their food. Get everyone back into their small groups; then tell the groups that from now until you say so, no one except you can talk. Distribute picnic materials to each group: bread, peanut butter, jelly, utensils, drinks, cups, and cookies. Then give them these rules: (1) No one can talk. (2) No one can prepare his or her own food. (3) No one can eat food by themselves—someone has to serve it to them. For an added challenge, crowd each group onto a small picnic blanket or make them sit within a staked-off area outside.

EXTRA
Blind Follow-the-Leader

Get enough blindfolds for at least half of your group. Have students form pairs or trios. One person in each group should blindfold the other (or others) and lead them around the church or outside for five minutes. They can switch roles for the trip back. When following, they should walk with just one hand on the leader's shoulder and follow his or her instructions.

Silent Picnic
5 MINUTES